ELIZABETH I
& THE SPANISH ARMADA

By
Colin Hynson

School Specialty
Publishing

Columbus, Ohio

Elizabeth I *The daughter of Henry VIII and Anne Boleyn, Elizabeth was born in 1533. She did not become queen until she was 25. As queen, she led England to victory over the Spanish. By the time of her death in 1603, she had won the respect and admiration of her people, and England was seen as a world power.*

Philip II *As king of Spain and a strong Catholic, Philip II hoped to unite his country with England by marrying Elizabeth I. She refused his hand in marriage and his attempts to convert her to Catholicism. As revenge, he built a huge fleet of ships, called the* Armada, *and attacked England.*

Sir Francis Drake *An adventurous explorer and pirate, Drake had Queen Elizabeth's favor. His actions, which included robbing Spanish ships, brought him great fame. In 1581, Elizabeth knighted Drake as recognition for the wealth he had brought to England.*

Duke of Medina Sidonia *As commander of the Spanish Armada, the duke was in charge during one of the worst navy disasters in Spanish history. He tried to conquer England with 138 ships and returned home two months later with about 70.*

Pope Sixtus V *The pope was a powerful and wealthy man. Philip II of Spain convinced the head of the Catholic church to join Spain against England. Sixtus V declared a Catholic crusade against England. Shortly afterward, the Armada sailed to England, where it was defeated.*

Lord Howard of Effingham *A clever politician, Howard was very popular with Elizabeth. He was promoted from commander of England's navy to lord lieutenant general of England. With Drake at his side, he defeated the Spanish Armada.*

Copyright © ticktock Entertainment Ltd. 2006 First published in Great Britain in 2006 by ticktock Media Ltd., Unit 2, Orchard Business Centre, North Farm Road, Tunbridge Wells, Kent, TN2 3XF. This edition published in 2006 by School Specialty Publishing, a member of the School Specialty Family. Send all inquiries to School Specialty Publishing, 8720 Orion Place, Columbus, OH 43240.
Hardback ISBN 0-7696-4703-0 Paperback ISBN 0-7696-4629-8
1 2 3 4 5 6 7 8 9 10 TTM 10 09 08 07 06
Printed in China.

CONTENTS

ELIZABETH COMES TO POWER 4
• *Catholics and Protestants* • *Queen Mary's death* • *Elizabeth, the heir*
• *Philip II's empire* • *Aztec gold*

ELIZABETH AND DRAKE 8
• *Francis Drake* • *Spanish treasure* • *Around the world voyage*
• *Trouble in the Netherlands* • *English assistance and Spanish anger*
• *The pope's help* • *Mary's execution*

PREPARING FOR THE ARMADA 16
• *Building the Armada* • *English warships* • *Sir John Hawkins*
• *Attack at Cadiz* • *English victory*

THE ARMADA SETS SAIL 20
• *Leaving Lisbon* • *Into a storm* • *Corunna*
• *Toward England* • *Fire beacons* • *First battles* • *Fireships*

THE BATTLE OF GRAVELINES 32
• *Making plans* • *Fighting at Gravelines* • *Medina's decision* • *Sailing North*

TOWARD THE END 38
• *Troops at Tilbury* • *Elizabeth at Tilbury*
• *Rough seas around Scotland and Ireland*
• *Starving sailors* • *Failure*

TIMELINE & DID YOU KNOW? 44

GLOSSARY 46

INDEX 48

ELIZABETH COMES TO POWER

In July 1553, Mary Tudor, a Catholic, became queen of England as Mary I. She insisted that her subjects followed her religion. Protestants were burned at the stake for refusing to accept the Catholic faith.

During the 1580s, Spain's King Philip II controlled a large empire around the world.

NORTH AMERICA

ASIA

AFRICA

SOUTH AMERICA

Spain's empire

With just 500 men, the Spanish explorer Hernan Cortes defeated the Aztec empire of Central America.

They have no armor or swords. We can crush them easily!

How can we defeat these men with their weapons?

Cortes took Montezuma, the leader of the Aztecs, hostage and demanded gold. The Aztecs fought back but were defeated.

I demand all of the gold in your city. Then, I will let you go.

You cannot hold me like this.

The Aztec wealth was sent to Spain from Mexico. This new wealth helped make Spain the most powerful kingdom in Europe.

With all of this gold, we will be able to defeat our Protestant enemies at home.

Yes, and we will also be greatly rewarded.

FAST FACT Spanish treasure ships did not sail alone. They sailed in fleets of between 30 and 90 ships. Two fleets sailed to Spain each year.

ELIZABETH AND DRAKE

Queen Elizabeth I watched the growing power of Spain with envy and fear. She wanted control of the wealth that Spain was gaining. In 1577, she summoned the sailor Francis Drake to her.

Mr. Drake, I will pay for your ships to attack the Spanish, but our agreement must be a secret. I cannot risk war with Spain.

Your Majesty, my ships will return loaded with treasures for your glory.

Drake set sail and attacked the Spanish treasure ships.

That was easy. The Spanish did not expect us to attack.

We should continue our voyage and find new treasure for Her Majesty.

Philip II controlled a Protestant part of Europe, called the Netherlands. They wanted to be free of Spanish rule. In 1572, the people of the Netherlands begin to fight their Spanish rulers.

The Dutch rebels fought hard, but they needed help. They looked to Elizabeth I, the Protestant queen.

Elizabeth I sent the Earl of Leicester with an army to fight the Spanish.

Fight on! Drive the Spanish from this country.

In London, Elizabeth I read an update about the rebellion.

If we can keep this rebellion going, then the Spanish will ignore my kingdom.

In Madrid, Philip II also read about the rebellion.

The cursed English. I must crush this Protestant queen now.

FAST FACT The Dutch Revolt lasted from 1568 to 1648. The revolt is also called the *Eighty Years' War*.

Philip II began planning an invasion of England. He needed the help of Pope Sixtus V. He sent Olivarez, his ambassdor to the pope, to Rome to speak with the pope.

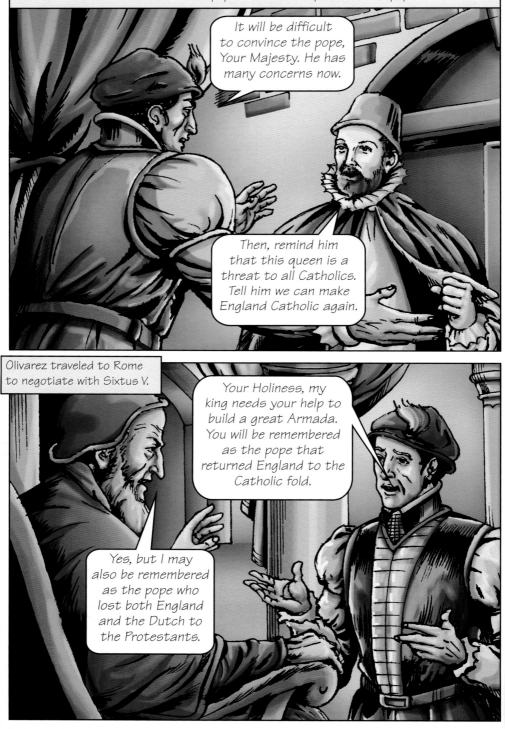

Olivarez convinced Sixtus V to help by telling him that the English Catholics would rise up in revolt once the Armada set sail. Olivarez was wrong, and the expected revolt never happened. The English Catholics remained loyal to their queen.

For our Spanish brothers.

For a Catholic England.

Down with the Protestant queen.

Olivarez returned to Madrid.

My lord, the pope agrees to help pay for the Armada, but only after we have overthrown Elizabeth.

FAST FACT Sixtus V finished the dome at St. Peter's Basilica and rebuilt much of Rome while he was pope.

In 1561, Elizabeth I's cousin, Mary, returned to Scotland as its queen. She was a Catholic and wanted to make Scotland Catholic again. She was also seen by many as the rightful queen of England.

Your Majesty, your return to Scotland is most welcome.

Thank you, Father. I pray that all of my people will join me in the true faith.

However, Scottish nobles did not want a Catholic Scotland. They began to plot against her.

She has married the Catholic Lord Darnley.

We must stop her. Will you join us and rise up against her?

Although Mary managed to defeat this rebellion, she was suspected in a plot to murder her husband. The Scottish nobles imprisoned the man she wanted to marry. In 1568, Mary was forced to seek help from Elizabeth I.

Mary was held prisoner by Elizabeth for nearly twenty years. Elizabeth knew that Mary was a threat to her throne, but she could not bring herself to execute a queen. It was only after a plot to assassinate Elizabeth was discovered in 1586 that Mary was tried and executed.

Mary was planning to kill our queen. To protect our country, she must die.

Mary is meeting her death like a true queen.

News of Mary's execution reached Madrid.

Your Majesty, the queen of Scotland is dead, murdered by Elizabeth!

Now, we must ready the Armada to avenge her death and restore the Catholic faith in England.

I wonder what the Spanish will do now.

PREPARING FOR THE ARMADA

The English knew that they had to slow down the preparations of the Armada so that they could prepare their defenses. In April 1587, Drake was sent to Cadiz for a surprise attack on the Spanish fleet.

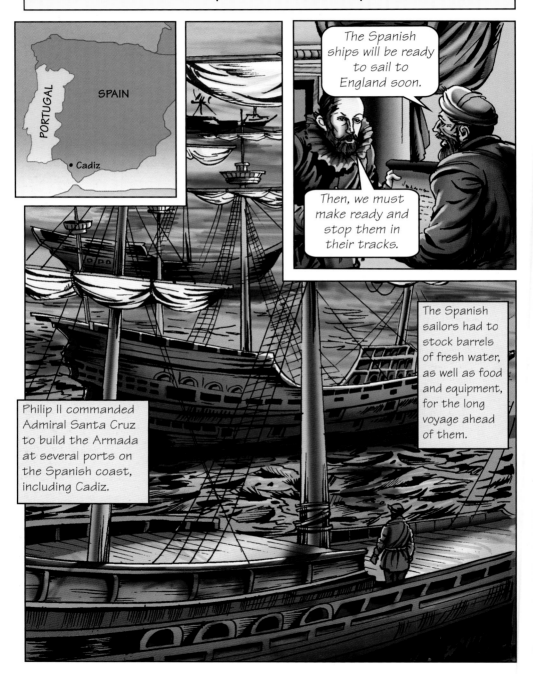

PORTUGAL

SPAIN

• Cadiz

The Spanish ships will be ready to sail to England soon.

Then, we must make ready and stop them in their tracks.

The Spanish sailors had to stock barrels of fresh water, as well as food and equipment, for the long voyage ahead of them.

Philip II commanded Admiral Santa Cruz to build the Armada at several ports on the Spanish coast, including Cadiz.

The English had begun to build a new kind of warship. These ships were smaller, faster, and better armed than the Spanish ships.

The English naval commander, Sir John Hawkins, was responsible for building the new ships.

Your Majesty, I am honored, but I get seasick easily.

We will never defeat the Spanish with more ships. We must rely on speed and agility.

Santa Cruz died in February 1588 before the Armada was ready. Philip II appointed Medina Sidonia to take his place. Sidonia did not want the job.

The English cannons were more powerful than the Spanish cannons. Drake could fire at Spain's ships from a safe distance.

Steady, lads! Wait until I give the order to fire.

Tell the men to keep their distance. The Spanish ships must be kept far away from us.

Drake destroyed nearly 40 of the Spanish ships that were preparing to join the Armada. His actions delayed the Armada by a year.

Fire!

A hit! We've been hit!

Along with the ships, the Spanish also lost valuable supplies, including barrels of fresh water.

FAST FACT Drake captured and looted the *San Felipe*. The *San Felipe* was one of the largest ships in the Spanish navy. It was loaded with gold, jewels, and spices. The cargo was valued at $200,000—a huge amount of money then.

THE ARMADA SETS SAIL

The Armada finally set sail in May 1588. It took two days for all of the ships to leave their ports. Medina Sidonia watched the ships sail away to sea. He was on one of the last ships to leave.

I have done all that I can. This great battle now begins. Soon, we shall have a great victory over the English.

News of the first sighting of the Spanish Armada reached England. An alarm was sent along the coast using a series of fire beacons.

Captain! I can see a fire in the distance. The English know that we are here.

Sir Francis Drake was playing a game at Plymouth when he was told the Armada was approaching. He seemed unconcerned.

Sir Francis, you must come quickly! The Spanish fleet has been seen sailing this way!

There is no need to hurry. We can finish this game and beat the Spanish, too.

FAST FACT Each fire beacon had one watchman. The watchmen were not allowed to have dogs, as they were seen as a distraction.

On July 21, the English and Spanish ships fought their first skirmish. Little damage was done by either side. However, the Spanish suffered their first loss when gunpowder on the *San Salvador* exploded. The *San Salvador* was badly damaged.

Medina Sidonia had to decide what to do.

We must take the supplies from the San Salvador and leave the ship. It is too badly damaged.

On the same day, the *Rosario* collided with another Spanish ship, causing heavy damage. Sidonia had to leave another ship behind.

Let's make it the first Spanish ship to sail to the bottom of the sea!

The *Rosario* was a tempting target for Sir Francis Drake. He commanded some English ships to leave the fleet and attack the *Rosario*.

However, Martin Frobisher, one of the commanders of the English fleet, was not pleased with Drake's decision.

He should have stayed with the rest of our ships. He is nothing but a pirate at heart.

FAST FACT The *Rosario* was one of the biggest ships in the Spanish Armada. It had 46 cannons and 300 soldiers.

25

On July 21, the Spanish fleet managed to organize itself. It formed a giant crescent-shape over 7 miles long. This formation made it very difficult for the English ships to attack.

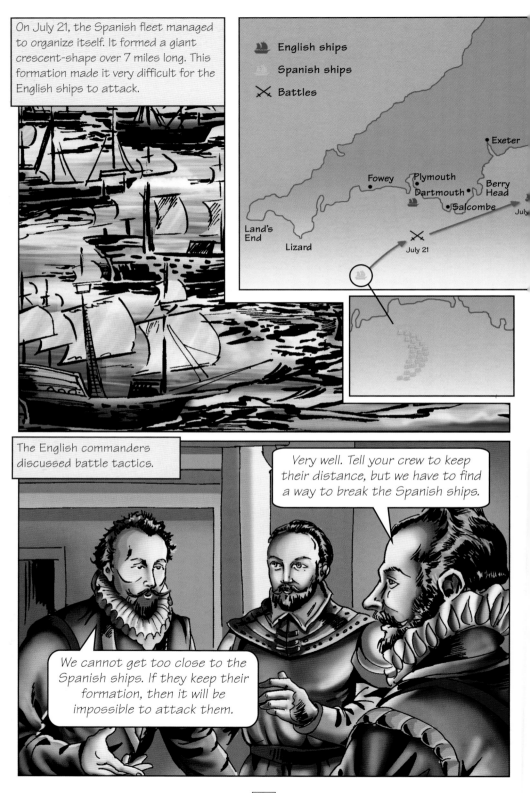

English ships

Spanish ships

Battles

Exeter

Fowey

Plymouth

Dartmouth

Berry Head

Salcombe

Land's End

Lizard

July 21

July

The English commanders discussed battle tactics.

Very well. Tell your crew to keep their distance, but we have to find a way to break the Spanish ships.

We cannot get too close to the Spanish ships. If they keep their formation, then it will be impossible to attack them.

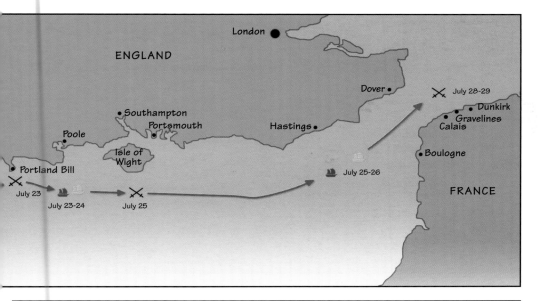

ENGLAND

London

Dover

July 28-29

Dunkirk
Gravelines
Calais

Southampton
Portsmouth

Hastings

Boulogne

Poole

Isle of
Wight

FRANCE

Portland Bill

July 25-26

July 23

July 23-24

July 25

The Spanish and English ships skirmished at Portland Bill on July 23. Two days later, they fought off the Isle of Wright. Neither side was able to gain the upper hand.

Remember, lads, keep your distance from those Spanish ships.

But we're too far away. We can't hit them at this distance.

FAST FACT The Spanish crescent was formed with the strongest ships on the outside and the weakest ships in the middle.

On July 26, Medina Sidonia sent a message to the Duke of Parma, who was waiting with Spanish troops to be taken across the English Channel and invade England.

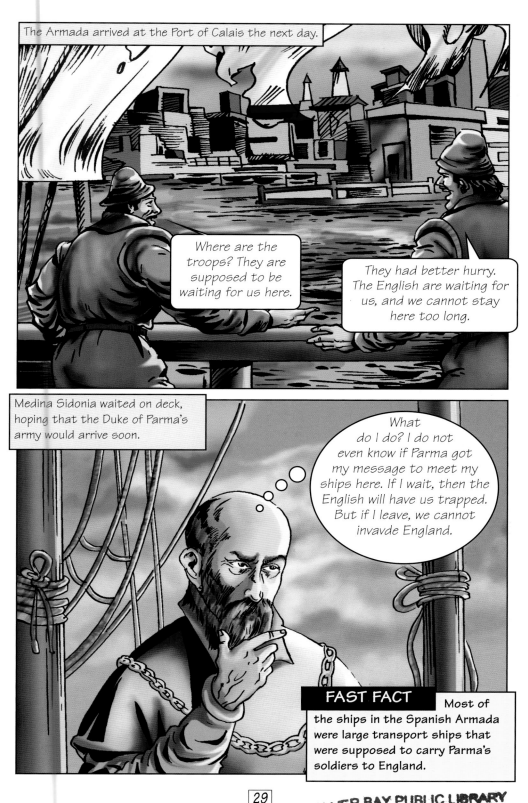

The Armada arrived at the Port of Calais the next day.

Where are the troops? They are supposed to be waiting for us here.

They had better hurry. The English are waiting for us, and we cannot stay here too long.

Medina Sidonia waited on deck, hoping that the Duke of Parma's army would arrive soon.

What do I do? I do not even know if Parma got my message to meet my ships here. If I wait, then the English will have us trapped. But if I leave, we cannot invavde England.

FAST FACT Most of the ships in the Spanish Armada were large transport ships that were supposed to carry Parma's soldiers to England.

29

On July 28, the English commanders decided to send in the fireships. Fireships were old ships that were set on fire and sailed toward enemy ships.

How many ships are we sending in?

Eight. The Spanish will panic and sail out of Calais, and we will be waiting for them. All we need to do is fill these ships with pitch and gunpowder.

The fireships were sent toward the Spanish ships. The Spanish reacted by using long hooks to push the ships away. At first, they were successful.

The fireships were filled with gunpowder and cannon balls. The gunpowder exploded, and the Spanish panicked. They sailed out of Calais in disarray.

Look out! It's heading straight for us. Raise the sails! Raise the sails!

FAST FACT Both the English and Spanish used fireships. The Spanish used them to try to stop Francis Drake's raid on Cadiz.

THE BATTLE OF GRAVELINES

With the Armada out of Calais and the Spanish fleet scattered, the English commanders had to decide on their next move. Drake, Frobisher, Hawkins, and Howard met to plan their strategy.

Supplies on the English ships were running dangerously low.

There's not much left. How can we fight the Spanish without weapons?

Put the ammunition there, lads.

More English ships arrived, and they were split into four groups.

Yes, my lord. Now they must listen to our needs.

You must take this message to England at once. All of our ships are low on cannon balls. I cannot fight the Spanish with empty guns.

Lord Howard was very worried about the lack of ammunition. He had already asked for extra supplies, but all of his messages had been ignored.

FAST FACT The English fleet had 2,000 cannons. The Spanish fleet had a total of 1,000 cannons.

On July 29, a major battle between the Spanish and English began at Gravelines on the Dutch coast. The English ships sailed close to the Armada, which allowed their powerful guns to have an effect.

The Spanish ships tried to sail closer to the English ships, so the Spanish sailors could board and overpower the English ships. But the Spanish were unable to reach them.

Aaargh!

Don't come any closer! Otherwise, you will taste English bullets!

The wind is pushing us northward. The English ships cannot be captured, and we have lost several of our own. Without Parma's army, we can do nothing. Order your ships to sail around this country and back to Spain.

Medina Sidonia saw that the Spanish could not win this battle. The Armada had to sail into the North Sea.

This is truly a sad day for Spain.

FAST FACT The large, slow Spanish ships used slaves as rowers.

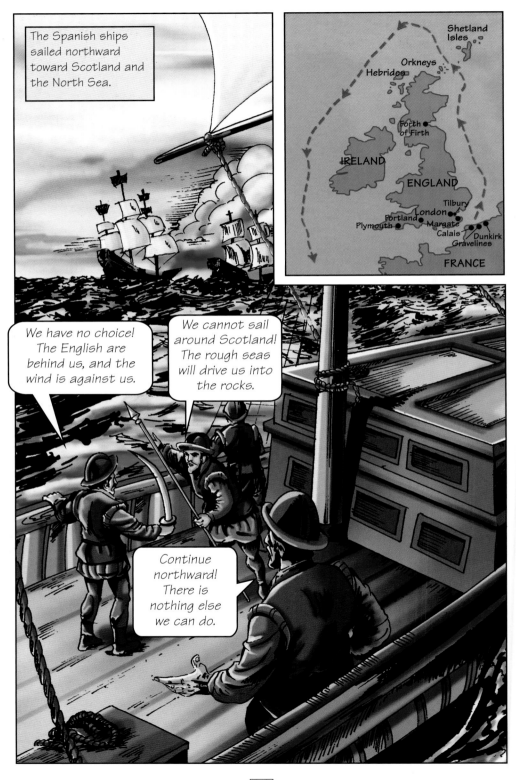

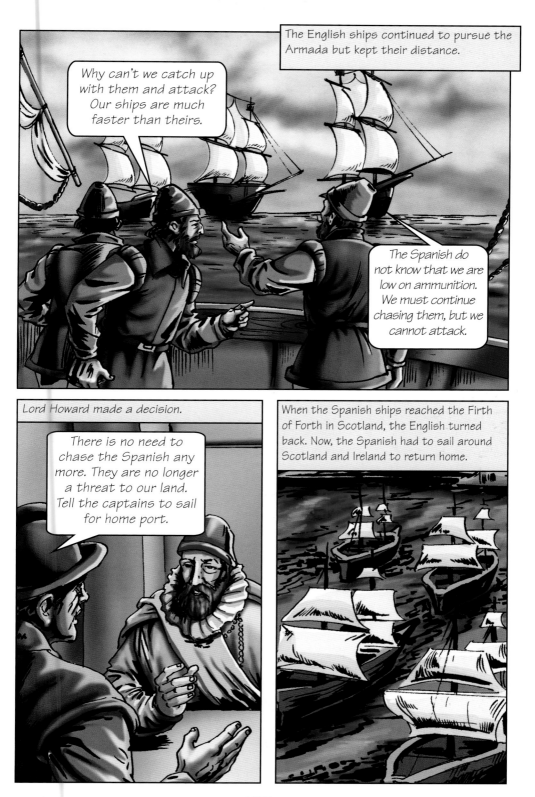

TOWARD THE END

While the Spanish ships were being chased toward Scotland, English troops at Tilbury waited for news. Despite being advised to stay in London for her own safety, Elizabeth I insisted on meeting her troops.

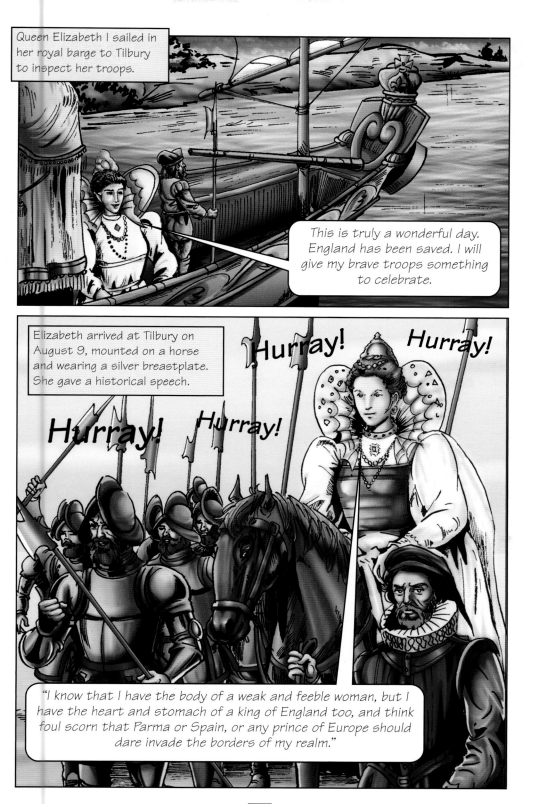

Queen Elizabeth I sailed in her royal barge to Tilbury to inspect her troops.

This is truly a wonderful day. England has been saved. I will give my brave troops something to celebrate.

Elizabeth arrived at Tilbury on August 9, mounted on a horse and wearing a silver breastplate. She gave a historical speech.

Hurray! Hurray! Hurray! Hurray!

"I know that I have the body of a weak and feeble woman, but I have the heart and stomach of a king of England too, and think foul scorn that Parma or Spain, or any prince of Europe should dare invade the borders of my realm."

Meanwhile, the Spanish sailors knew that they faced new perils by traveling around Ireland and Scotland.

The English ships have stopped chasing us.

Yes, but they have left us to the dangerous seas around Scotland and Ireland. We might not survive the voyage home.

Sidonia was warned about the stormy seas. He was also given some more bad news.

My lord, the supplies are running low. We have very little fresh water and not enough food to go around.

The men are already tired and dispirited. We must keep this from them for as long as possible.

The Spanish sailors soon found out that they were running out of food and water, so they took drastic action.

What are you doing? Those horses belong to the king. You cannot throw them overboard.

What use are they now? We cannot use them to fight the English. They are drinking our water.

Throw them over the side.

FAST FACT Three Spanish ships tried to sail to Norway. They were never seen again.

The Armada sailed into the Atlantic Ocean. Storms scattered the fleet, and the Spanish crews became more exhausted and hungry.

We should be enjoying the spoils of victory in London, not fighting for our lives in this storm.

Nearly all the food and water is gone. What are we going to do?

The Armada captains did not have any maps of the western Irish coast. They did not know about the treacherous rocks that awaited them. Many ships were wrecked. Many Spanish soldiers that made it to shore were hunted down by the Irish.

Run for your lives! I have heard that the Irish show little mercy to foreigners!

Spaniards! Over there! Don't let them get away!

The battered remains of the Armada arrived home on September 20, 1588.

Can those ships really be the same that sailed away nearly two months ago?

Yes, it is true. Our magnificent fleet has been defeated.

We were told that victory was certain.

Medina Sidonia begged Philip II to be relieved of his command. King Philip II allowed him to retire and did not blame him for the failure of the Armada. The Spanish never seriously threatened England again.

FAST FACT More than 1/3 of the Armada was lost at sea. Over 20,000 Spanish sailors and soldiers lost their lives.

Elizabeth I, often referred to by her subjects as the *Virgin Queen*, was one of the longest reigning monarchs of England. During the 45 years of her reign, she managed to transform England into a powerful nation with a large empire.

1556: *Philip II becomes king of Spain and the Netherlands.*

1558: *Elizabeth I becomes queen of England.*

1562: *Elizabeth I gets smallpox and nearly dies.*

1564: *William Shakespeare is born.*

1565: *Tobacco is first brought to England. Lord Robert Darnley becomes king of Scotland and marries Mary, Queen of Scots.*

1567: *Lord Darnley is murdered.*

1568: *Mary, Queen of Scots, flees to England in exile.*

1577: *Francis Drake sails around the world.*

1580: *Drake returns to England after circumnavigating the world.*

1581: *Francis Drake is knighted.*

1583: *John Somerville attempts to assassinate Elizabeth I.*

1584: *Walter Raleigh establishes a colony in Virginia.*

1585: *Elizabeth sends an army to help the Dutch fight the Spanish.*

February 1587: *The execution of Mary, Queen of Scots.*

April 1587: *Drake attacks the Spanish ships at Cadiz.*

May 1588: *The Spanish Armada sets sail from Lisbon, Portugal.*

May 30, 1588: *The Spanish Armada finally sets sail for England.*

July 19, 1588: *The Spanish Armada is sighted from the English coast.*

July 21, 1588: *The Armada enters the English Channel.*

July 23, 1588: *The two sides fight near Portland Bill.*

July 25, 1588: *The two sides fight off the Isle of Wight.*

July 27, 1588: *The Spanish Armada anchors off the port of Calais.*

July 28, 1588: *The English send in fireships. The Armada is scattered.*

July 29, 1588: *The Battle of Gravelines.*

July 30, 1588: *The Armada begins to sail north.*

August 9, 1588: *Elizabeth I gives a speech to her troops at Tilbury.*

August 12, 1588: *The English ships stop chasing the Armada.*

September 20, 1588: *The Armada arrives back in Spain.*

1593: *Battle of Ballishannon.*

1596: *Sir Francis Drake dies.*

1601: *Elizabeth delivers her* Golden Speech.

1603: *Elizabeth I dies. James I becomes king of England.*

DID YOU KNOW?

1. There were more Spanish Armadas launched against England after 1588. They all had varying degrees of success, but none conquered England.

2. Sidney Wignall was the first person to explore a sunken Spanish Armada ship. In 1968, he located and studied the Santa Maria de la Rosa.

3. One month after Mary I died and Elizabeth took the English throne, Philip II proposed marriage to Elizabeth.

4. Philip II was a very religious man. He would pray between three to four hours everyday.

5. Parma's army in the Netherlands was only about 18% Spanish. The rest were either Germans or Italians.

6. The Spanish sailors were given one bottle of wine and three pints of water a day. The water had to be used for both drinking and cooking.

7. The Armada took enough wine to last six months. However, most of it was undrinkable and useless.

8. As well as all of the other ammunition, the Spanish Armada took 120,000 bullets with them to invade England.

9. The men who worked the beacons

were not allowed to have chairs. This was so they would not sit down and fell asleep on duty.

10. At the beginning of 1588, Charles Howard, the commander of the English fleet, believed that the Spanish would land in Scotland and invade England from the north.

11. The English sailors were given a gallon of beer a day to drink instead of water.

12. When Elizabeth spoke to her troops at Tilbury, she was smiling so much that many people saw that her teeth were black.

13. On Sunday, December 4, 1588, there was a special celebration at St. Paul's Cathedral to celebrate the English victory.

14. Six hundred Spanish sailors were shipwrecked on the coast of Scotland. They were treated well and returned to Spain.

15. Punishment on board both Spanish and English ships was harsh. Any sailor found guilty of murder was tied to the body of his victim and thrown overboard.

16. The first English person to see the Spanish Armada was the captain of the Golden Hinde, *Thomas Fleming*.

17. The English ships did not have enough ammunition. England had quickly used up most of the materials available in the country to prepare for the Spanish Armada's attack. The whole country nearly ran out of ammunition.

GLOSSARY

Armada: *A large group of ships used in battles during strategic warfare (see also* **Formation***).*

Barge: *A large row boat used to tow large vessels out to sea. They were used by both sides to move their ships out of port.*

Beacon: *A way of communicating over long distances with the help of light or fire. Usually, this signal represented a warning or alarm.*

Broadside: *When all of the cannons on one side of the ship are fired at the same time.*

Catholic: *A member of the Catholic church, e.g. King Philip II.*

Circumnavigate: *A term to describe a vessel that travels around something. Francis Drake circumnavigated the world between 1577–1580.*

Coronation: *The ceremony in which a king or queen is crowned.*

Decks: *The flooring of a ship. Most ships had more than one deck. These included the main deck and the upper deck.*

Draft: *The amount of water needed to float a ship.*

Execute: *To kill someone as a punishment for a severe crime. In Elizabethan times, the criminal was usually beheaded.*

Flagship: *The ship that carried the navy's commander.*

Fireships: *Old ships that were set on fire and sailed toward an enemy ship. Both the Spanish and the English used fireships in battle.*

Formation: *When something is put into a particular order and shape. For example, the crescent formation of the Spanish Armada.*

Frigate: *A small ship used by the Spanish to protect their treasure ships.*

GLOSSARY

Galleon: *A large ship used by the Spanish. It had guns on the main and upper decks.*

Hulk: *A large vessel that was intended to transport cargo for short distances. The Spanish Armada used them to carry troops over to England.*

Pope: *Leader of the Roman Catholic Church, who was very influential and wealthy.*

Protestant: *A Christian who belongs to the Protestant church, e.g. Queen Elizabeth I.*

Race-built galleons: *The name of a new, fast ship designed by John Hawkins.*

Skirmish: *Irregular or spontaneous fighting.*

Successor: *Somebody who follows another in a position. For example, a ruler or a commander of a ship.*

Smallpox: *A disease that causes chills, fever, and a rash. If it is not treated quickly, it can lead to death.*

Stake: *A large wooden pole that was used in executions. Victims were tied to it and burned alive.*

Traitor: *Someone who betrays their friends or country. In Elizabethan times, a person who betrayed their country would most likely be executed (see **Execute**).*

Treaties: *A formal agreement between two or more countries.*

Treasure ships: *Large ships used by the Spanish to bring gold and other valuables from Central and South America to Spain.*

Wreck: *When a ship is either destroyed, abandoned after hitting a rock, or sailing into a storm.*

INDEX

ammunition 33, 37, 45

Armada 46
> preparation 16–19
> setting sail 20–31
> toward the end 38–43

Aztecs 6–7

Battle of Gravelines 32–37

beacons 23, 45, 46

Cadiz, Spain 16–19, 31

California 9

cannons 19, 33

Catholics 4–5, 12–15, 46

Cortes, Hernan 6

Drake, Sir Francis 2, 8–9, 16–19, 23, 32

Dutch Revolt 10–11

Effingham, Lord Howard of 2, 32, 37

Eighty Years' War 11

Elizabeth I 2
> Dutch Revolt 11
> end of the Armada 38–39
> Francis Drake 8–9
> timeline 44

England
> battles with Spain 22–37
> first attack on Armada 18
> Philip II's invasion 12–13
> warships 17

executions 4, 15, 46

fireships 30–31, 46

Fleming, Thomas 45

food supplies 9, 16, 40–42

Frobisher, Martin 25, 32

gunpowder 4, 24, 31

Hawkins, Sir John 17, 32

Ireland 42

Leicester, Earl of 11

Mary I 4–5

Mary, Queen of Scots 14–15

Netherlands 10–11

Norway 41

Olivarez 12–13

Parma, Duke of 28–29

Philip II 2
> Armada 16–17, 43
> Dutch Revolt 10–11
> invasion of England 12–13
> marriage to Mary I 5
> religion 45
> Spanish empire 6

Pope 2, 12–13, 47

Protestants 4–5, 47

Rosario 25

sailors 9, 43, 45

San Felipe 19

San Salvador 24

Santa Cruz, Admiral 16–17

Scotland 14–15, 36–37

ships
> numbers in Armada 21
> transport ships 29
> treasure ships 7, 8, 47
> warships 17

shipwrecks 42, 45, 47

Sidonia, Medina 2
> appointment as commander 17
> Armada 20, 24–25, 28–29, 35, 40
> retirement 43

Sixtus V, Pope 2, 12–13

skirmishes 24, 27, 47

Spanish Armada
> see Armada

Spanish empire 6–7

storms 21

tactics 26–27

Tilbury, England 38–39

transport ships 29

treasure ships 7, 8, 47

warships 17

water supplies 16, 19, 40–42

Wignall, Sidney 45

wine 45